Read: [*v*] The act of interpreting and understanding language, symbols, and the written word.

Furiously: [*adv*] To do something with excitement and passion.

Read Often. Read Well.
Read Furiously

On my mind this morning:
no competition
no blame.

~ Lao Tzu

One 'n Done #14

Sipping a Cloud

Poems by
Kathy Kremins

Published by

For all my teachers:
human
and
more-than-human

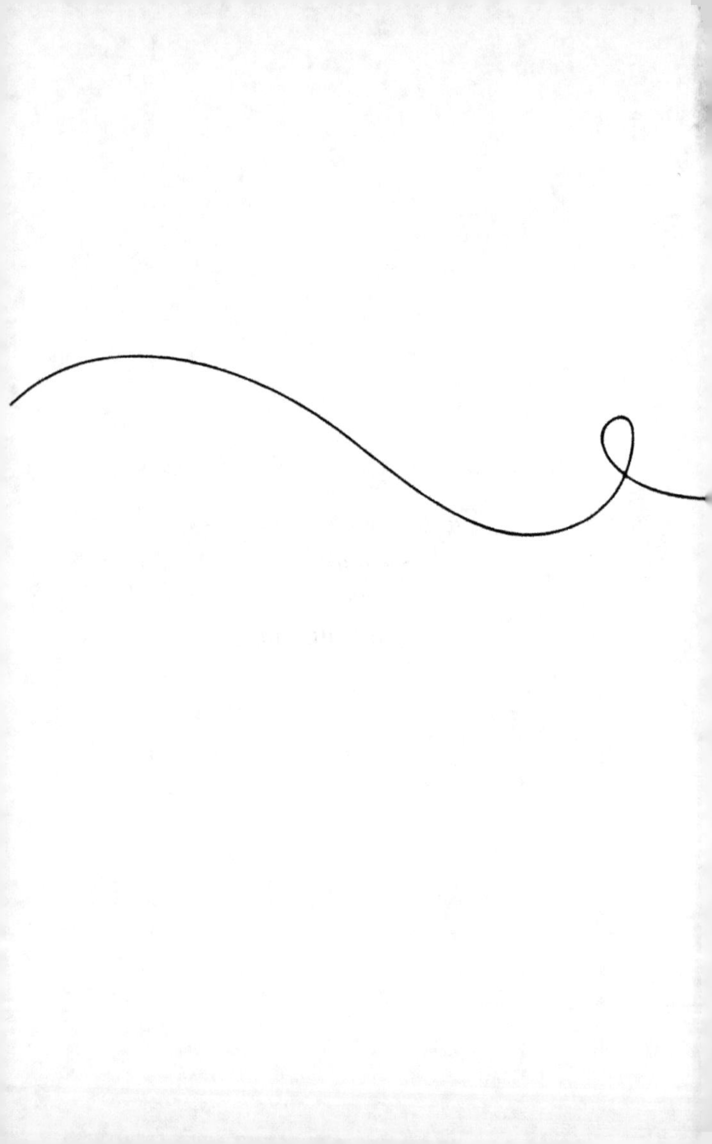

All of the poems and prose in this collection were written between September 29, 2023, and June 8, 2024. While most were written specifically for this project, some work insisted on joining the *Sipping a Cloud* sangha.

Rather than reaching for my phone to take a picture, write a haiku.

~Clark Strand

If you want to know the weather, go outside.

~Someone whose name I have forgotten

I write when I walk, so this introduction has been through more iterations than I can begin to count. As a matter of fact, this book has been in many forms and genres and speculations since Sam approached me with the proposal to write a book for Read Furiously and their One 'n Done series. Of course, I jumped at the opportunity, and after a wide-ranging and inspiring conversation with Sam, I grabbed a bunch of balls and started juggling. When someone gives you total freedom, you have to play and take some risks.

My initial thought was to try something new-ish, to work in a way that I wasn't comfortable, and to challenge myself not only with form but also content. After two chapbooks and a full-length collection, I thought prose might be what I needed to tackle. But as I worked, I realized that I was rewriting those poems as memoir, so a few of the balls started bouncing. Something in the rhythm of the bouncing balls, as well as something Sam mentioned in our conversations, was writing a hybrid work. So I grabbed a few new balls while managing not to drop the couple I still kept airborne.

A decade ago, I spent ten months living by the

ocean on the Jersey shore. I retired early from teaching to write full-time. What I found myself doing was running a yoga studio, teaching some classes, and making a mess of my life. Living by the ocean was a gift (literally) to find a space to do the writing I wanted to do and heal myself. But I couldn't find my way back to a writing habit while I managed to put myself back together again with three-times-daily long walks on the beach.

Luckily, early in my stay, I had a fortuitous conversation with my beautiful friend, Alexander Rosenberg. Alex is a master glassblower (and one of the best humans I know). On a visit to the shore house, we had a multiple-day conversation on creativity, process versus product, having a practice, and many other things (with an emphasis on doodle dogs, specifically Seamus and Cleo, our respective rescues). As an athlete, coach, yoga teacher, and yoga practitioner, practice was very much a part of my daily routine. Until Alex explained that he blew glass every day to maintain the skills he possesses so he could then work longer and in more detail, I hadn't correlated it to practicing poetry every day.

So for those ten months in Manasquan, after

my first cup of coffee and a walk along the beach in all kinds of weather (including a few monumental snowstorms and nor 'easters), I wrote haikus, tankas, and a short form of my creation called matins. These very specific forms kept me focused on craft and attention. As a practice, it allowed for repetition and imagination while I sipped my coffee and wrote poems. It kept me in the present and expanded all possibilities. And provided a structure to repair my life. That practice has joined me in many moves and lives since then.

After dropping many of the balls of potential book ideas and themes, I wound up holding three that I hadn't dropped: mindfulness, my haiku/tanka practice, and silence. So, with much gratitude for Sam's permission to explore, to my meditation teacher, Jean Vitrano, and to the Dharmakaya Retreat Center for quiet space, this little book has come to be. May it find a home in you and be a faithful companion while you sip your clouds.

Two crows on maple tree
Pileated woodpecker claims
Fall sunrise for all

Shadows

There are openings in our lives
of which we know nothing.

An old dog on the porch
barely lifts its white muzzle
but those eyes of wide greeting
like the face of you, dear one
shifts the shadows in a day.

Both moment of contentment
and moment of loss.

Reminded that a heart
unloved is still a heart
as a cup unfilled for years
is still a cup.

Asters hold yellow
Tight, letting go for later
Early fall too soon.

Hawk wings shadow glide
Over pine and autumn ground
Ignore me, tasteless.

Autumn morning bright
Just-past full moon hangs lightly
Dew twinkles, fireflies.

Cast of clouds gather
Sky above soon-falling leaves
Room for all of us

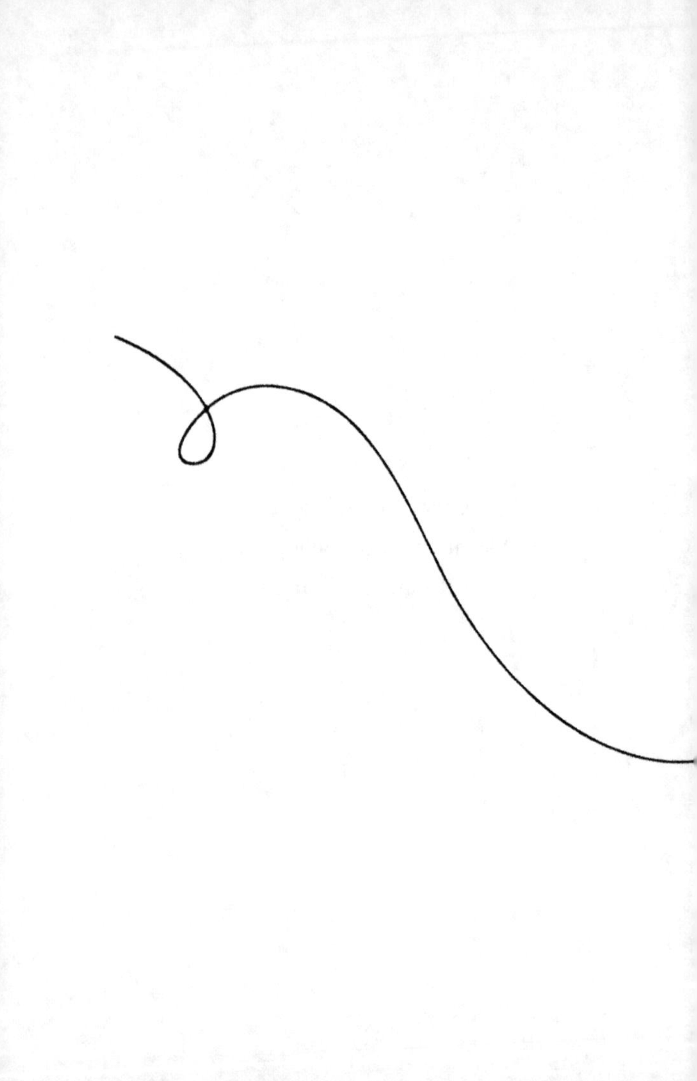

My mother was fast with everything: cooking, cleaning, talking, walking, ironing, working, and gardening. What slowed my mother down and allowed her to stop was tea. My mom even prayed fast. But a cup of tea was a way for her to be still, slow, settled. And she sipped. This woman who could drink a glass of water in two gulps often took two hours to finish her tea, which was long gone cold.

It was ritual, perhaps a reminder of the old country, the warmth of peat fire, a sense of safety, and a memory of belonging. But it was also a tool for conversation and connection, whether with her sisters in the kitchen, with my father on a Sunday morning as he had coffee and she listened to him read the paper and the articles and comics that might interest her, or with my Dad's sister, Aunt Betty, on the front porch in summer on Alexander St. gossiping about the neighbors and periodically yelling at us kids to be careful of the cars and warnings to not break windows. There was also frequent laughter, of which I was never privy to the content.

A cup of tea gave my mom permission to pause. To touch the present moment with a tenderness and lightness that she didn't often feel. It gave her the stillness so she could feel the love and care in her life. Sipping her tea gave her brief clarity into the goodness of her immediate world that too often was buried in a sad, lonely past and flooded with worry for an uncertain future for her queer child, her husband with PTSD and a fragile heart, and limited financial resources.

Sipping a cup of tea was a balm.

Rains came, washed out
All the haikus written here.
The lesson: what is.

I Want to Write a Long Poem

I want to write a long poem about you
make a conceit out of nervous gentle brushes of your
hands
capture in a word how you scrunch your mouth when
you receive a compliment
squint of eyes and tilt of head when a dog licks your
cheek

build similes from studying your lower lip approaching
the rim of coffee cup
     like a slow kiss glacier melting
memorizing your slender fingers tender in touch of a
body glass or a poem
     as a dancer glides with control of wild abandon

walking beside you through smiling sunflowers at
twilight
alliteration of freshly flush fragrance
echo of longing flooded with assonance
sonics of bird song whistling tune of sunrise

but mostly I want to stay in this poem long enough to
jettison my fear that
        loving you with these lines changes us

draws us to edge of desert
stops us from entering cathedral of ascent to endless
sky   untouchable horizon
clarity of the unknown
I want to be still with you in a poem with only
beginnings

Maple and ash drop leaves
Like rain. With eyes closed, beware
Squirrels throw acorns.

Shower of acorns
Intermittent woes this day.
Do not flinch. Be still.

So lost in deep thought
Disoriented in the forest
Three steps back, clarity.

Frost's Elves

She is all pine and I am apple orchard.
What I bear and how she pierces
entertains the elves, pilfering stones
for the wall the neighbors mend every Spring.

Wee folk make the best neighbors where
everything is a game without an outcome
endless play, laughing at our seriousness
amused at our demand for space we don't own
where possession is an oppressive illusion
sense of control is the ultimate hilarious prank.

As little people pluck rocks and trees jostle
over Mother Earth's unclaimed property
they turn Lao Tzu into a lilting sing-song:
No competition; no blame.

No competition; they sniff the pine.
No blame; they eat the apples.
They steal stones without guilt or regret.
She and I never mend.

Learning How to Float

waiting for hands to hold me
to trust enough to relax
to go deep, underwater
eyes and mouth closed
ears rushing with the plummet
water, sensation, panic
flailing begins, I see, I taste
gasping for breaths

the near drownings wither me
such lessons in dying
disguised as life, desire
when all along I needed
to believe I would be held up
if I only learned how to let go

Aligned with the North Star
Crow sits on dead ash, deep black
Against pale blue sky

Lying awake last night, thinking about writing this contemplation, my heart hurt. No. My heart was missing. In its place was a canyon in my chest, echoing, "lonely lonely." How profoundly lonely my Aunt Mary must have been. She was old, frail, and hunched from my earliest memories when she would have been in her mid-forties.

A seamstress in a Newark clothing factory, a reader of tea leaves, an obsessive buyer of unneeded items, a loser-of-her-way on city buses, a drinker of cheap wine where it, and she, hid in the attic, every night she pulled out the love seat into a single bed where she slept in the living of our two bedroom apartment occupied by five people.

Aunt Mary didn't want to come to America, but post-war Ireland was a land of economic hardship. She and my mom worked in Dublin as domestics and barely made ends meet. So when Aunt Bride and the Ryans sponsored them to the States, Aunt Mary was presented with an empty choice: be alone in her country - the Old Country- or be lonely in America.

She chose loneliness with her sisters.

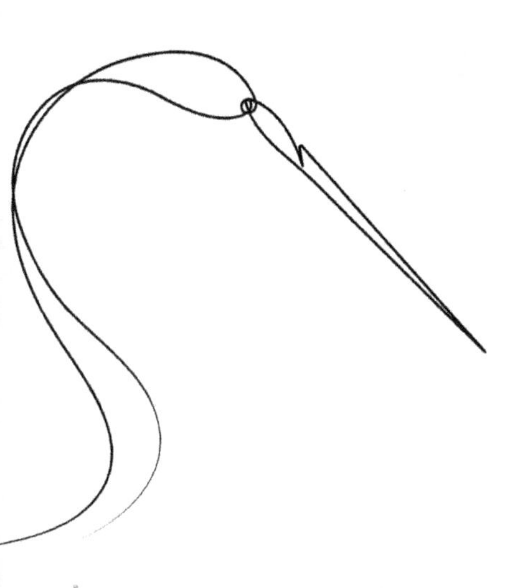

Lost breath of warm wind
Green, orange, gold, yellow
Change in the stillness.

Three birds call in fog
Questions without any answers
Let it be, let it be.

Slow walking, hands clasped
Salamander on the path
We both step softly.

Lone crow in treetop
Caw-caw-caw-caw to none and all
Four beat instructions

Water & Air
-for Amy

Rough presence airs the heart,
tender presence waters it.

How light we are with good company.

Giving and receiving unnoticed,
surprised by providence

like the sunrise photograph
of a half-frozen lake, above a bed, unmade.

Time of Golden Leaves
Flutter, sway, no destruction
Rain before the rain

But For the Silence

Prayer is lapis for intercession and contemplation, is reached
by travelling as far as possible east or west, up or down -

murach an tost

Poets were ten-a-penny in Ireland
everyone either knew one or was one

murach an tost

I was sure that he quit cold,
but heroin has a habit of warming white knuckles

murach an tost

I don't know, and won't now, and I lay there
in the empty bathtub thinking about that for awhile

murach an tost

with the urns, heavy old things, hugging them to me.
Live so that someone will miss you.

murach an tost

I understand it better, now. It has to go
somewhere. You have to let it out.

Poetry Ireland Review, Issue 139. The cento comprises lines from
the following poets in this issue: Doireann Ní Ghríofa, Shannon
Connor Winward, Emily Berry, Airea D. Matthews, Maria
Isakova-Bennett, and Nick Laird.

Making Eye Contact With the Bear In the Forest, or the Poet Sees Her Own Shadow

What to keep
What to leave behind

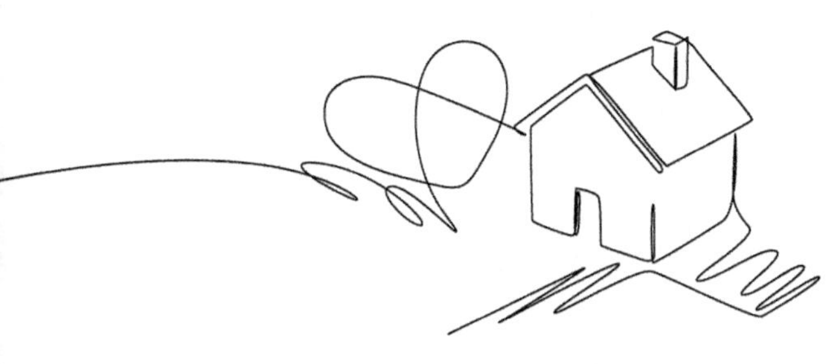

Heat Dome

Dear Neighbor,

The sprint is on to the wildest, spiraliest slide,
the kind that flips a small body every which way,
brings giggles and squeals, high squeaks
from skin burns that appear after hours of crazy runs.
The next sprint is to open field where the rolling
begins
races that twist and spin us into a dizzy band of old
young who finally sit on slightly wet asses
eat snacks off grass-stained knees. We smell
like earth, damp, warm, and mellow.

So when do we become enemies to ourselves,
grow into efficient, performance-based nuisances,
playfulness left behind in that old park traded
for an artificial turf field on the lower income
side of town, so your important adult schedule
of drinks with friends, facials, pickleball, date nights
are not interrupted by late-spring thunderstorms
that cancels soccer practice and ruins not only
this day but tomorrow as well. You pay coaching fees

for pleasure and taxes for convenience.

Dear neighbor, we are not friends, but I ask that you
consider not voting for those politicians who value
your precious time and resources over the precious
health of the children and elderly, as well as
the more-than-human on the other side of town.
I come from a people who existed in kinship with
other beings and the natural world. Let's return
not to something old but to something being born,
a promise whispered by ancestors. Be quiet and listen.

With wise hope,
Your neighbor on THAT side of town

Maslow's Hierarchy of Needs
Flipped and Revised
By This Woman Wielding a Pen
Who Happens to Be a Buddhist

may we all have clean air, healthy food, consistent shelter
    weather-appropriate clothing, and solid sleep

may we all have a living wage, a reliable support system
    affordable health care, and a place to call home

may we all experience a web of kinship with each other
    interconnectedness with the more-than-human
    world,
    and a sense of belonging

may we all participate in the Beloved Community, gift
economy,
    and the currency of gratitude and reciprocity

may we all have peace

Holy shit! Morning
Take a photo with your eyes
Peregrine falcon.

Caterpillar, breeze
Shifts eyes momentarily
Back to green beauty.

Pungent odor lurks
Better to smell than to see
Beware hidden skunk.

Finger of winter
On my shoulder, a few flakes
Tap lightly for now

Do I step around
Pools of water, storm falls hard
Wet feet are the path.

Birds fly with the wind
Leaves flip themselves, beat in ease
Surrender sometimes.

Droplets shivering
Held between the ribs of leaf
To hold oneself so.

We only had one bathroom (tub, no shower) for four adults and a preteen/teen me in that two-bedroom apartment. We also knew that between 7:30 and 8:15 was Aunt Bridie's spa time. Luckily, I was allowed in since I always needed to pee a lot. I have to say that despite how different Auntie and I were, we were also very much alike. I realized years later that my fascination with *Project Runway* was not because I have any sense of fashion (although Billie Eilish makes me feel good about my younger self) but rather because I appreciate attention, tenderness, care, and creativity.

That is what I witnessed as I finished peeing, stood up, closed the lid, and sat down again. I would watch a completely naked Aunt Bride - without any shame in either of us - wash herself (Ivory Bar soap and face cloth), put on body lotion (shea butter) as she massaged her legs and arms, smiling as she rubbed her "Buddha belly" (as she called it), and winking at me. As she set to tend to her face with Oil of Olay, we began to talk about our days. I asked her a lot of questions and received thoughtful answers, such as an "I don't know" or "What do you think?" Then, she put on her pink satin pajamas and wrapped toilet paper around her hair.

My mother of the short fuse, my Aunt of the long love. Non-patience, all-the-patience. Racing, stopping. Martyrdom, loving kindness. What lessons can be learned about moving through life on a toilet seat, studying the beauty and kindness of an older woman! May we all find those teachers who love us unconditionally and without attachment.

Evening mist predicts
What the mountain hides away
Rainy morning comes

Correcting Eliot

Eliot got it wrong - "April is the cruelest month" - or maybe climate change not only raised temperatures, warmed the oceans, killed species, increased drought, led to starvation, displacement, and poverty but also revised poetry. "March is the brutal month." Violent deaths, birthdays of beloveds lost to fear and addiction, and long loves faded from neglect. Dear One, I'm sure you know it has been a hard year, feel it in the shifts my body takes reshaping itself through rupture and repair. Like the shattered picture frame scattered at my feet, not thrown out of anger, just a slip from not being attentive, I have learned. Oh, how I learned! To pray the world in this poem, to praise the more-than-human for what they teach me, to not pretend that April may bring gifts my way, to pay forward the blessings of coffee and walks with you.

Grass sparkles, blade caresses
sunfilled rain, hand-blown droplets
such globes of wonder.

Earth, wind, fire, and air
Tumble in a sky bucket
Sunset blazes autumn.

A hard fog morning
Skeleton of branches
Finches sing of soon-spring.

Slimy and shiny
Frog escorted by three birds
No one is in charge.

The Voice In My Head

I am a verb   not a noun

    I am an action   not an object

   I am a process   not a category

     I am dynamic   not static

I am a journey   not a destination

       I am a home   not a house

     I am love   I am peace

         I am all beings

I am

A familiar path
Cut trail, moist earth, fallen trees
Never the same place

On slope of mountain
Dandelions gone to white
Waving like peace flags

The mountain reminds me
With a gust of its pine breath
How to build a home

The raindrops dancing
Wink, signaling to each other
Fireflies in daylight

What I Want My Body
to Tell You

that I loved my father, the ever-present cardinal,
diligent, whimsical, loyal, always a moment away from
song

        perched on my left ankle

that I'm rooted in traditions of prayers, blessings,
meditations, and contemplations

        right foot anchors to Mother Earth

that my Irish ancestors steer this boat of a body in
ancient Ogham, in Celtic symbols for community
and faithfulness, in the oppressed Irish language, not
killed, now rising

        Anam Cara

            Grá

that Seamus and his Smalls are the first beings
I'm reminded of every morning in the mirror, the
triskele braid weaving our permanent bond on this
impermanent body

chest open to the world
that my Littles, boys now, know a lightness of being
so they can see - as my father did but with less of
the pain - how love is written in parents' hands the
bedtime songs I sing and the Latin words I carry on
my fingers the world I want for you

Amor Mundi

Noli Timere

That men and women have been my family, my
friends, my lovers, kins of all kinds, tiny treasures,
markings of connections to the rivers flowing through
and between

neck, wrist, hip, ribs, sternum,

shoulders, triceps, biceps, forearms

That a landscape of trees and flowers bloom in my
aging like water reflecting this abundant garden, an
illuminated manuscript to be read and traced in what
remains of desire

back, upper arms

Who, how, what, and why I love is what my body will
tell you when I die

Clouds drift with no plans
Cold sky, a stream with no end
Floating with eyes closed

I have written poems about Dad gardening, especially on the day he died. I wasn't home. I was spending the weekend with my girlfriend, and we went to NYC, where I visited the Empire State Building for the first time at 22, even though I lived 5 miles away. I was probably on the journey back down to earth when Dad died on the couch with our dog beside him.

It was late April, and he was getting the garden ready. When I talked to him on the phone Friday night, he sounded tired, but he was excited about the beautiful weather, digging in the dirt, throwing the ball for Barney, and raking. I've never seen anyone love to rake as much as him. After a good, long chat (of which Patty joined us for some of it from the upstairs extension), Dad said, "I love you, Katie."

"I love you, Dad. Get some rest tonight. Lots to rake tomorrow," ending our phone call with a mutual chuckle.

There is comfort in small things. We said "I love you" always after our good nights. He called me by his nickname for me - "Katie." And we laughed. Lots. The movie I run through my head, created from all the memories of watching him, is his tender raking of the dead leaves from the flower beds, kneeling and scooping them with ungloved hands into the metal bin to be composted sometime later. But what brings the biggest smile to my face and tears to my eyes is when my mind-movie freezes on the moment when Dad draws the dirt-covered dried leaves under his nose, breathes deeply, then raises his face to the sun, grins, and exhales ever so slowly.

Field of lavender
as breeze blows across the hill
laughter fills my nose

Lost and Found

After days of solitude
a gift of being swallowed
taken in life like a lost kitten
from a mid-winter ice storm
holding a cup of hot tea
with the tips of fingers
admiring the solid blue pattern
you slide in, for a moment
the cup now your face
delicate, smiling, a wonder
my hands surround the warmth
drinking slowly, like kissing
the found kitten on the nose
like kissing you, almost, on the mouth.

Out of the Silence

These days too many words and not enough.
I kept you at a pandemic distance
Only to be caught by your smile after
Years hidden. I had forgotten its lift
Its dance, its whimsy, how your dark eyes matched
The playfulness of your peach-red lips
And your hair. Ah, how your black hair fell
Out of sight, only to return to match
your eyes. What I want from you is an honest word
What I will be is the hardest truth you've heard.

New trail is portal
To possibilities like
Prayer flags, my heart
Flutters to you, how we walk
In noble silence, words unneeded.

If these worms had arms
And legs, lost in ecstasy of rain
No need to save them.

No love in haiku
Is silly to me, inhale
Field of lavender.

Nothing lifted here
Sun and fog became good friends
Grass and trees clapped.

Do Not Apologize
for Your Tears

I have seen you here before
in a different body and another language.

You don't see me.

You sit on the bench in the clearing,
weeping quietly, but I know.

I feel it, too.

All that we can be, so close,
yet we can't quite hold onto it.

It always slips away.

But we keep coming back,
we know we hear it deep in the woods.

Peace   Peace   Peace

To Bee

Was this the first time I watched so long?
Settled on the rock so deep in the woods
while you hovered in a small patch of lavender
so calm, full of notice and ease,
I marvel at your navigation.

Then   *turbulence*
                    darting
flitting

WHIRLING

                              high

            turning

                              low

                                          SIDEWAYS

all ways except upside down

I'm caught in your chaos
off on a raucous ramble

Are we safe?
On a mission?
Drunk on scent and sound?
Lost?
Found?

Is this the erotic ecstasy of St. Theresa
or the sublime joy of this present moment
where I finally stay, attentive, still
in awe of the physics of flight?

A Monk in the Woods

Rinpoche, have I not seen you serving meals in the
cafeteria
>you and my plate, full of the local gardens' plenty
>and our smiles fueled by silence? There is
>something
>about a mouth as a beacon, even when words are
>not spoken.

the map is not the territory

Rinpoche, am I walking a fine line, approaching a thin
place
>so many thresholds waiting as I meditate in
>motion
>while you, in near distance, bend to cup the tulip?
>Eyes often view the same scene, but meaning
>rests
>in the act: you as savior, you as lover, you as child.

the map is not the territory

Rinpoche, how low you bend to place smooth river
rocks

    precariously balanced, this work of art - stone,
    hand, breath
    this dance - breath, hand, stone: this planting -
    hand, stone
    breath? Holding mine as I came upon you in the
    woods
    watching like a startled deer, all alert, all attention.
    Alive.

The map is not the territory

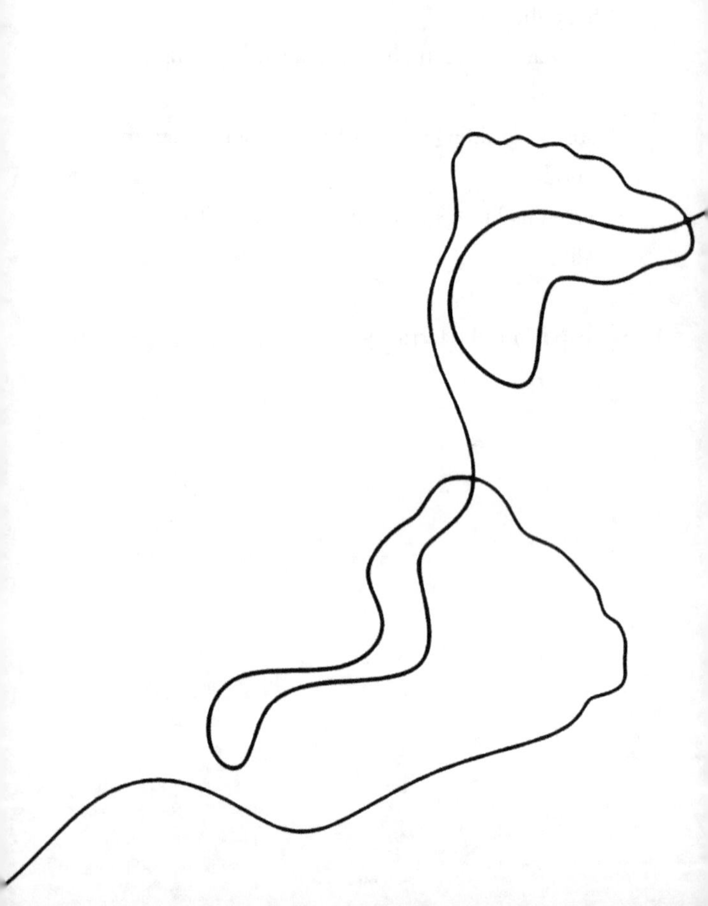

Ghazel for Poems
Lost on a Walk

I won't look at poems lost on a walk,
go back to the heart loaned on the walk.

Hand in a hand, prayer is not a promise
deep in the arboretum's domed walk.

Flowers and garbage depend on each other
like butterfly and magnolia on brick-sewn walk.

There is wisdom in blinking dust from eyes,
in nourishing freshness, not tomed walks.

To this woman in the woods, I see you
as a verb not a noun, as a loaming walk.

You followed me home
Up the mountain road, wings wide
Always a wonder.

Mid-May mountain mist
Walking, holding my own hand
Loyal companion.

Shit happens, life breaks
My heart into tiny shards
Cherry blossoms fall.

Windblown

Thoughts of you bounce
in each raindrop on the uneven sidewalk
smiling as I rock on the porch
try to catch your profile in the moment
before the water hits the stone
before I lose the image of this woman I long for.

It's just a phase, this desire,
for someone untouchable
turning from a tear to ocean

I study you as my attention
shifts to the wet fern
reaching through the porch slats
curled upward
stretched to the sky
catching rain

You may not notice
I always listen carefully to you
to the shape of words you gift me
from your tongue to my eyes

that knits them so thinly
they slip into vibrations of my heartbeat

If this desire is just a phase
I need to stop my imagining
move your windblown hair from your face
let your eyes see what I see

Wind and rain, sideways
Umbrella, me, inside out
No competition

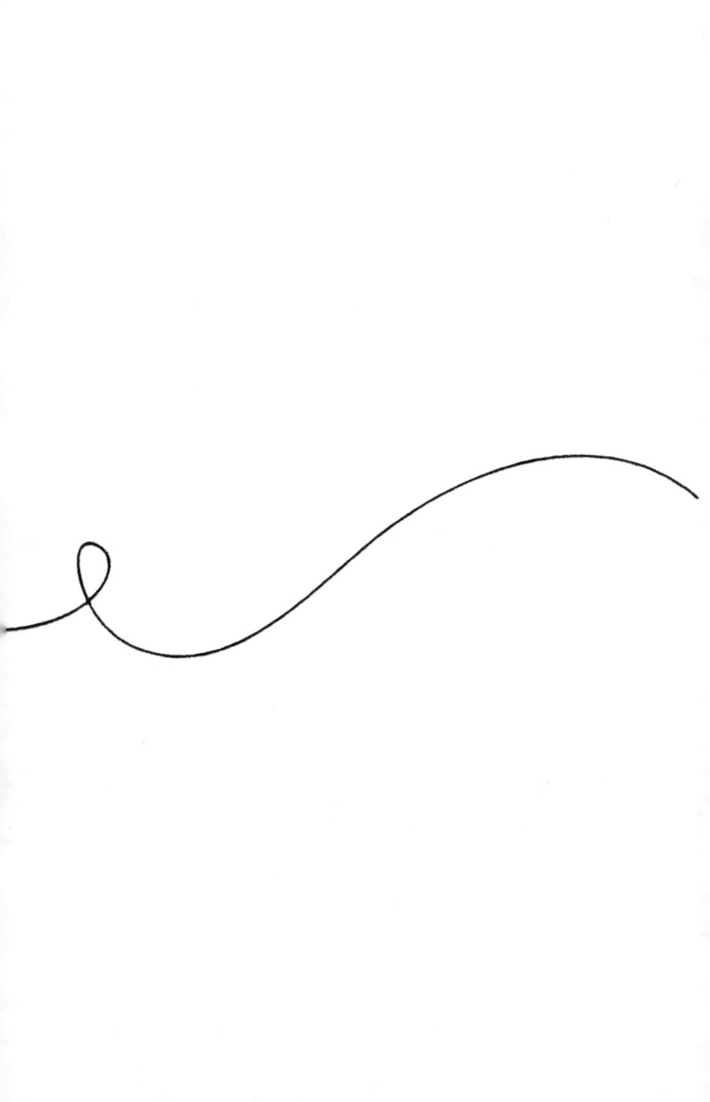

Gratitudes

For the publication of "Windblown" in *The Rutherford Red Wheelbarrow* #17.

For my Creative Partners: Adam Wilson, Samantha Atzeni, and the Read Furiously team. This book breathes because of your faith in me and my vision for it.

For the healers: Amy Leblanc, Debra Bernath, Eytan Kurland, Jean Vitrano, Jessica Yunker, Ramona Kelly, Signe Heffernan, and Zoe Bean.

For the poets: Ameerah Shabazz-Bilal, Attorious Renée Augustin, Claudia Cortese, Cord Moreski, Dimitri Reyes, Florence-Susanne Reppert, Gabriel Cleveland, Dr. Grisel Y. Acosta, Lynne McEniry, Marina Carreira, Nikki Carroll, Paula Neves, Rachelle Parker, Ras Heru Stewart, Rashad Wright, Rescue Poetix, Sam Rubenstein, Steve Zmijewski, Talena Lachelle Queen, Toma Zbrizher, and Ysabel Y. González.

For my kin (human): Dr. Anthony Di Battista, Alexander

Rosenberg, Bethany Shenise, Brenda DeRogatis, Denise Brown-Allen, Doug Farrand, Duncan Clegg, Elen Vittoria, Franz Vintschger, Patrick Wight, Jane Waddell, Jean Hughes, Kathy Kremins (the Original), Kelly Buwalda, Kim Helsel, Kristen Ames, Marianne Lloyd, Mary Jane Larkin, Matt Hanks, Melissa McHugh, Meredith Martin, Molly Rose Kaufman, Nan Ellis, Genevieve Brennan, Sarah Anderson, Sarah Klein, Sean McHugh, Sheila Kelleher, Shira Brown, Silver Cordero, Steve Vittoria, Suman Patnaik, Tom Corbo, and Wendy Hanks.

For my kin (more-than-human): Berry, Cherry, Daphne, Dutch, Elvis, Freddie, Horatio, Hazel, Heloise, Joni, and Yogi.

For my mindfulness sanghas: A Mindful Life Studio, Dharmakaya Center, and Plum Village.

For my writing spaces: General Store Shops & Cafe, Hilton House, and True Salvage Kitchen.

For my hearts: Arlo Clegg, Cate McHugh, Felix Clegg, and Kiera McHugh. I write for you.

About the Author

Kathy Kremins is a poet, photographer, and independent scholar. She is a retired NJ public school teacher and coach and holds a doctorate from Drew University. She has three poetry chapbooks: *Unrehearsed with Toma Zbrizher* (Two Key Customs, 2025), *Seamus & His Smalls* (Two Key Customs, 2023), and *Undressing the World* (Finishing Line Press, 2022). Her first full-length book of poetry, *The Curve of Things*, was published by CavanKerry Press in May 2024.

Her second collection, *Sipping a Cloud*, is forthcoming from Read Furiously in April 2026. She is the author of *An Ethics of Reading: The Broken Beauties of Toni Morrison, Nawal El Saadawi, and Arundhati Roy* (2010) and an essay contributor to *Too Smart to be Sentimental: Contemporary Irish American Women Writers* (2008). Kathy Kremins has also contributed to Read Furiously's New Jersey anthologies, *Stay Salty* and *Disco Fries & Scenic Drives*. She is also an editor for NJ Audubon Magazine.

Find Kathy Kremins online at: kathykremins.com

A Note to our Furious Readers

From all of us at Read Furiously, we hope you enjoyed our latest installment in our One 'n Done series, *Sipping a Cloud.*

We pledge to donate a portion of these book sales to causes that are special to Read Furiously. These causes are chosen with the intent to better the lives of others who are struggling to tell their own stories.

Reading is more than a passive activity – it is the opportunity to play an active role within our world. Each cause has been researched thoroughly, discussed openly, and voted upon carefully by our team of Read Furiously editors.

To find out more about who, what, why, and where Read Furiously lends its support, please visit our website at readfuriously.com/charity

Happy reading and giving, Furious Readers!

Read Often, Read Well,
Read Furiously!

More in the One 'n Done Series

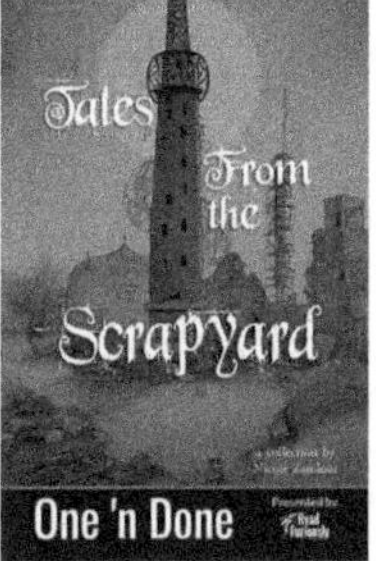

Small Books. Big Impact.
Learn more about the series at
readfuriously.com/one